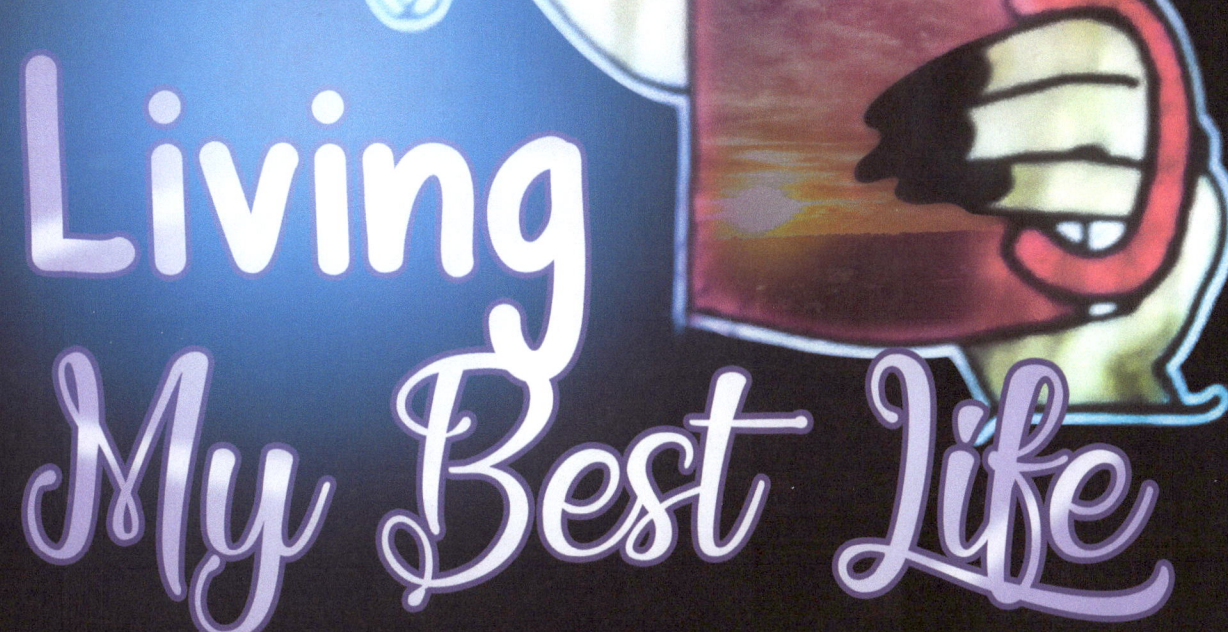

Author Alisa Saddler

November Girl Sunrises

Living My Best Life

Copyright © 2020 by Alisa Saddler. 821320

All rights reserved. No part of this book may be reproduced or transmitted in any form or by any means, electronic or mechanical, including photocopying, recording, or by any information storage and retrieval system, without permission in writing from the copyright owner.

To order additional copies of this book, contact:
Xlibris
844-714-8691
www.Xlibris.com
Orders@Xlibris.com

ISBN: Softcover   978-1-6641-3817-9
        EBook   978-1-6641-3816-2

Print information available on the last page

Rev. date: 10/20/2020

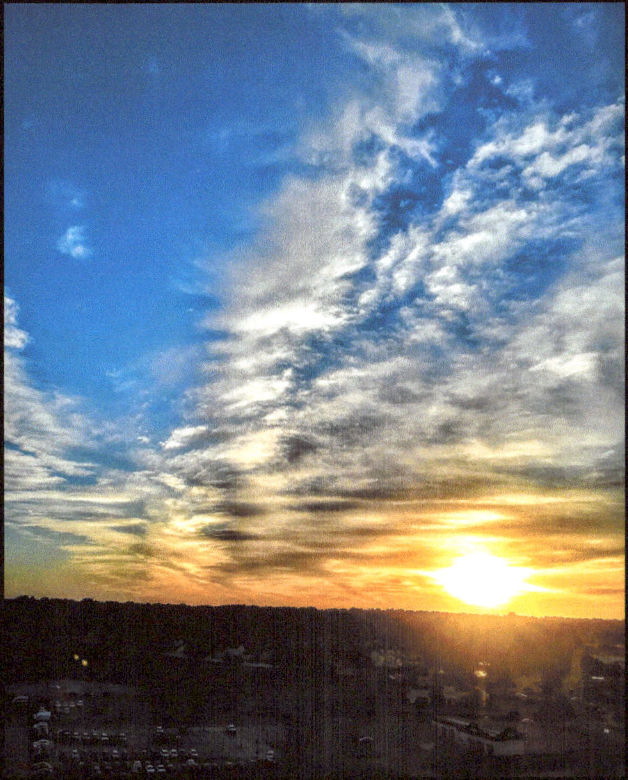

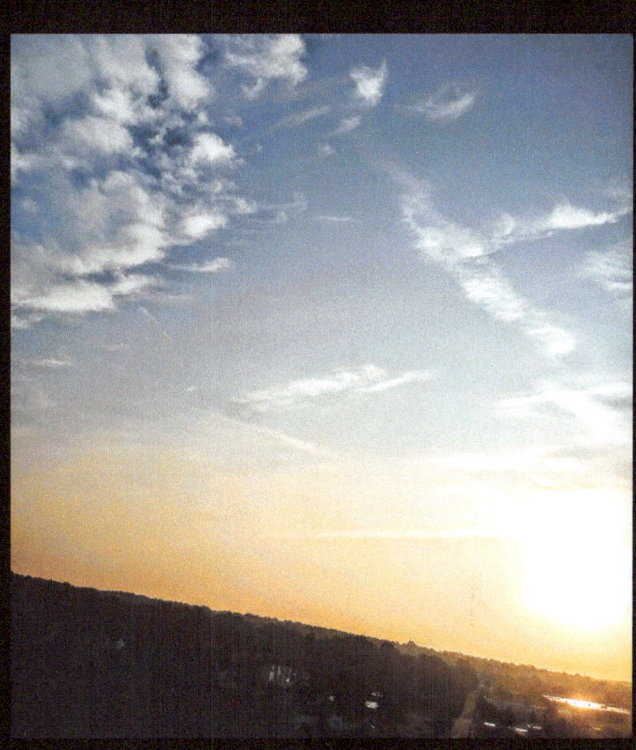

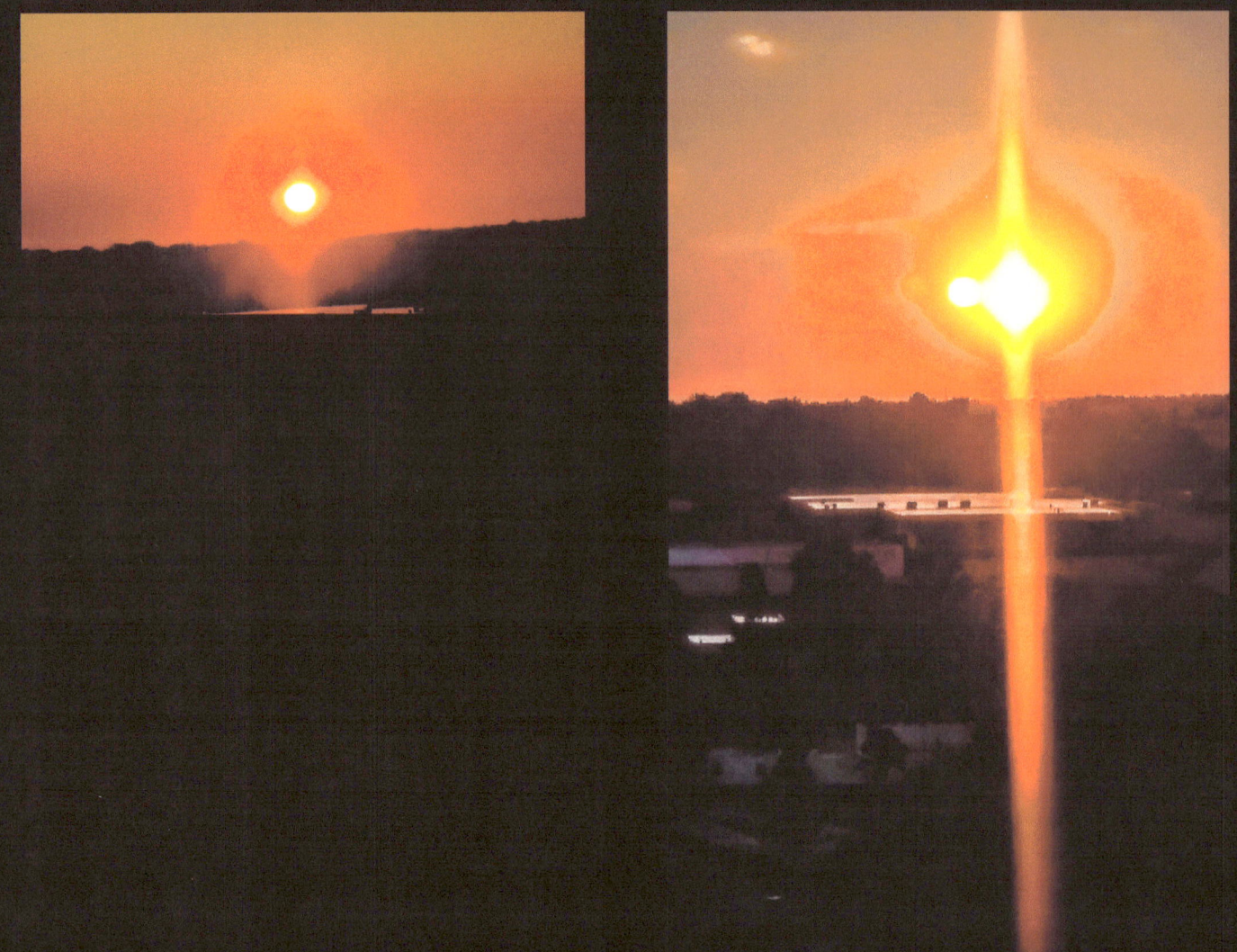

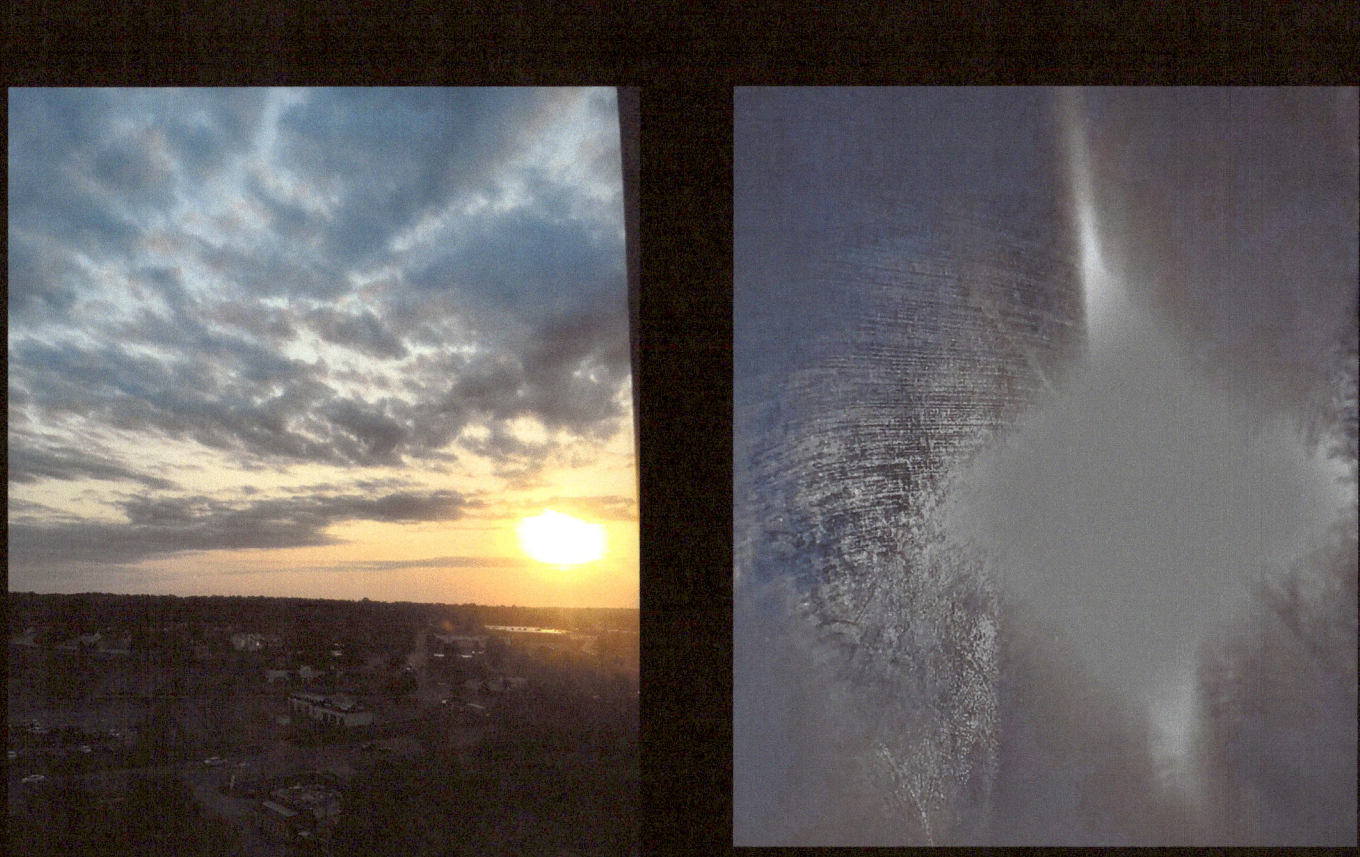

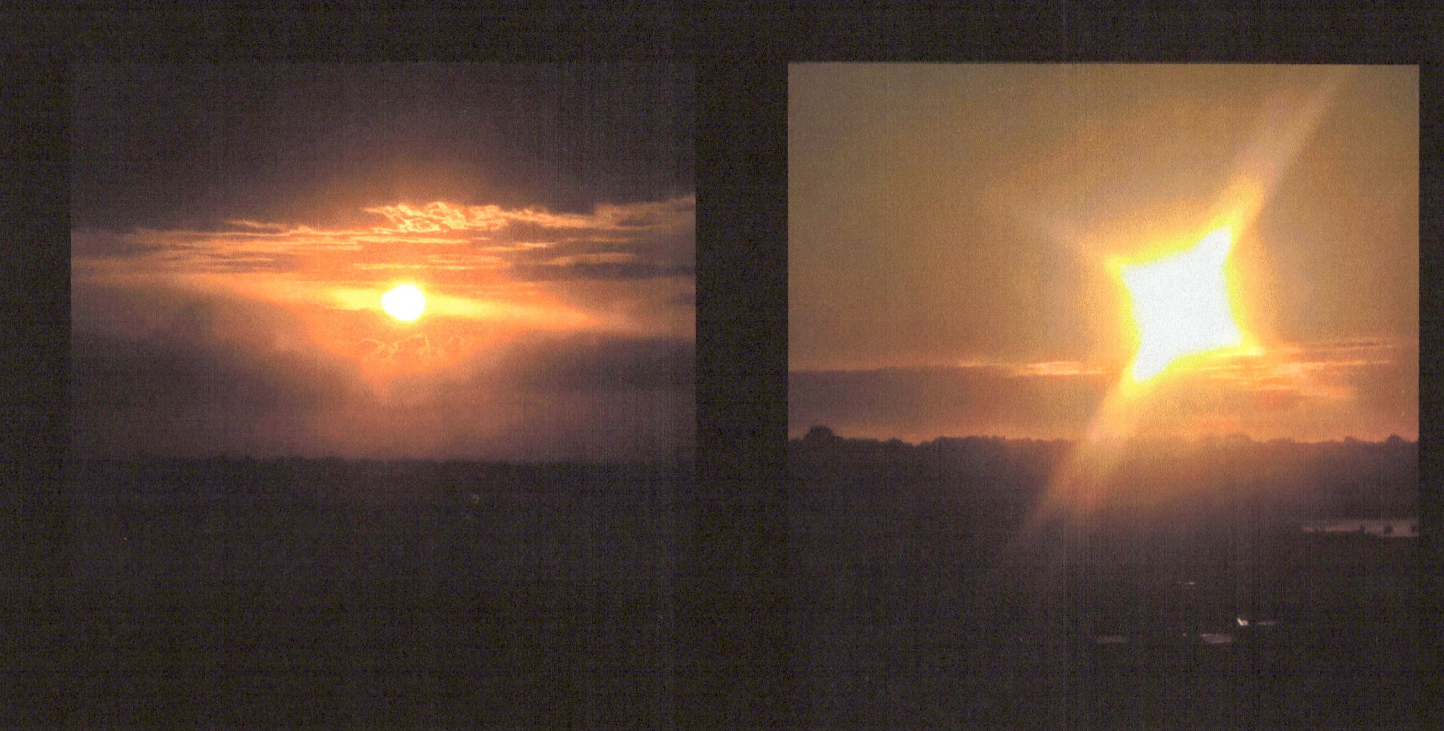

April

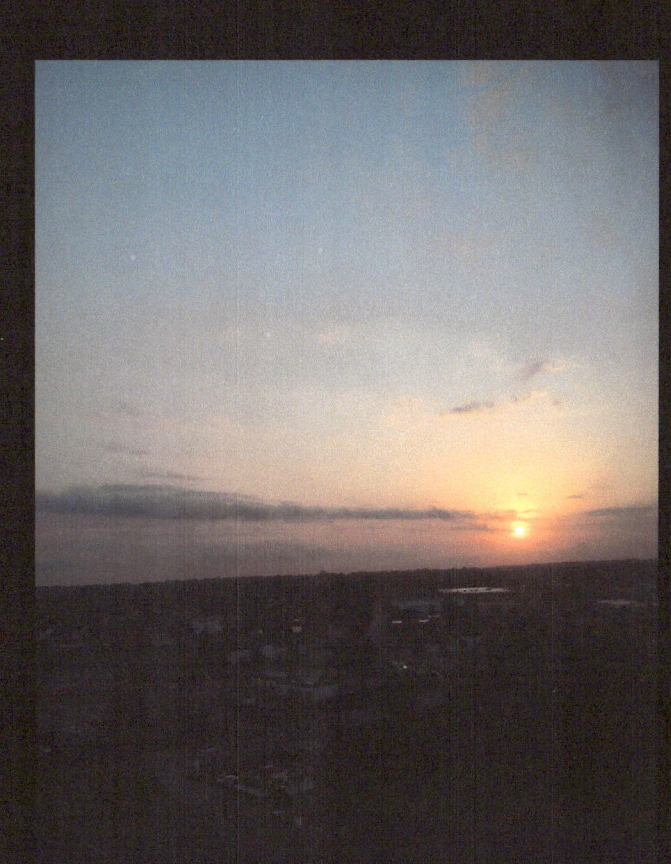

May

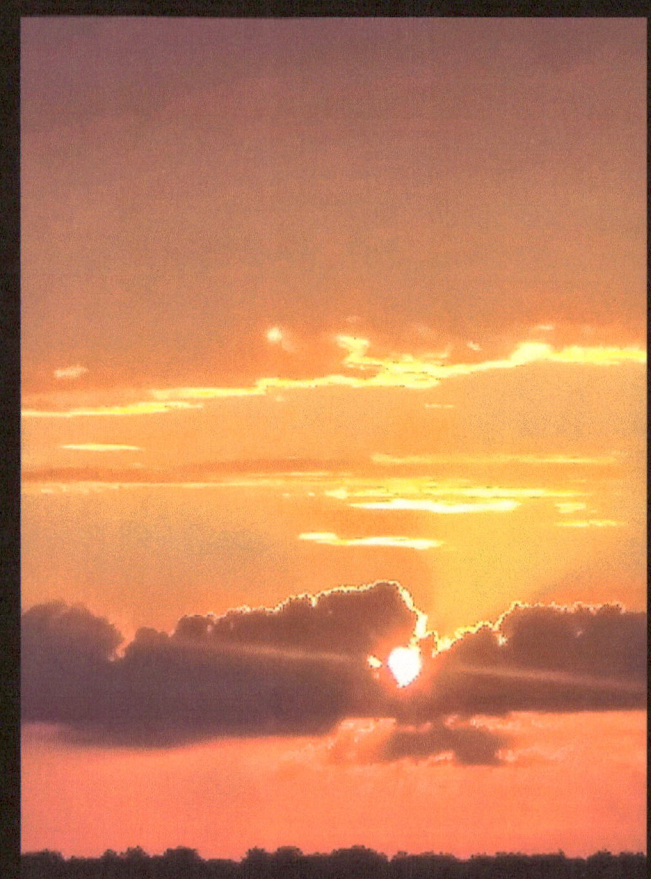
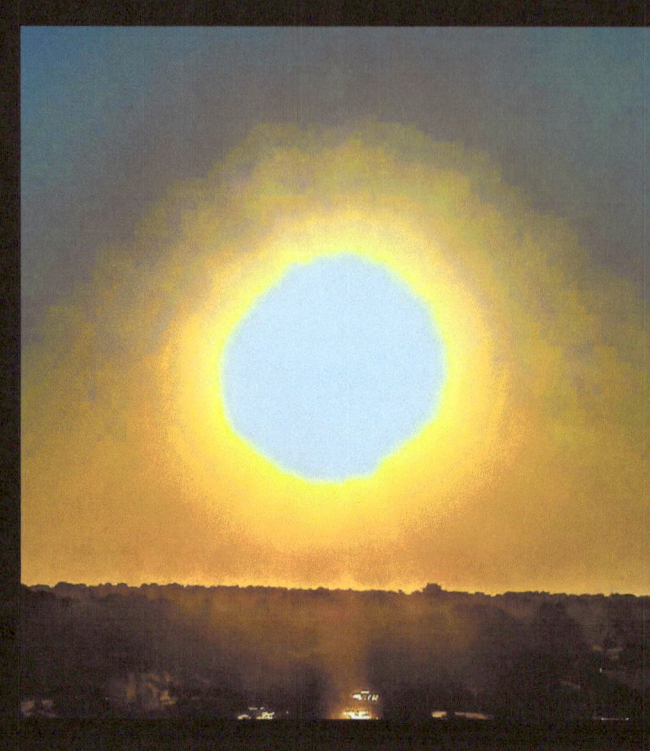

June

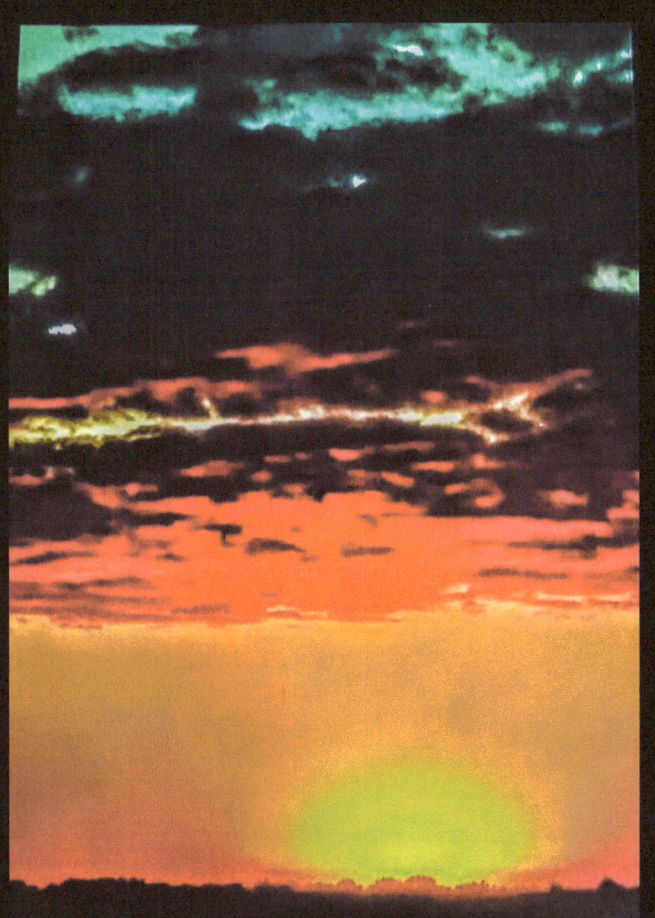
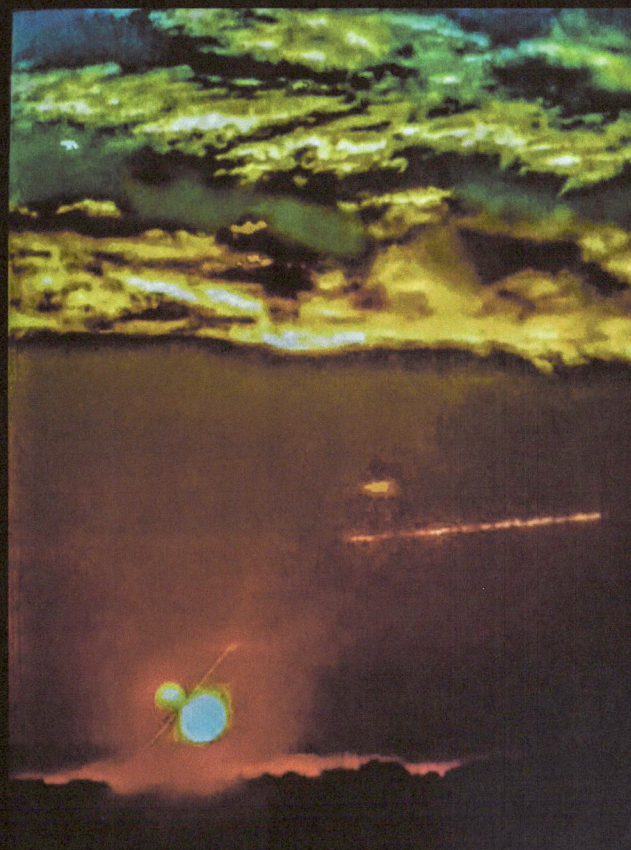

July

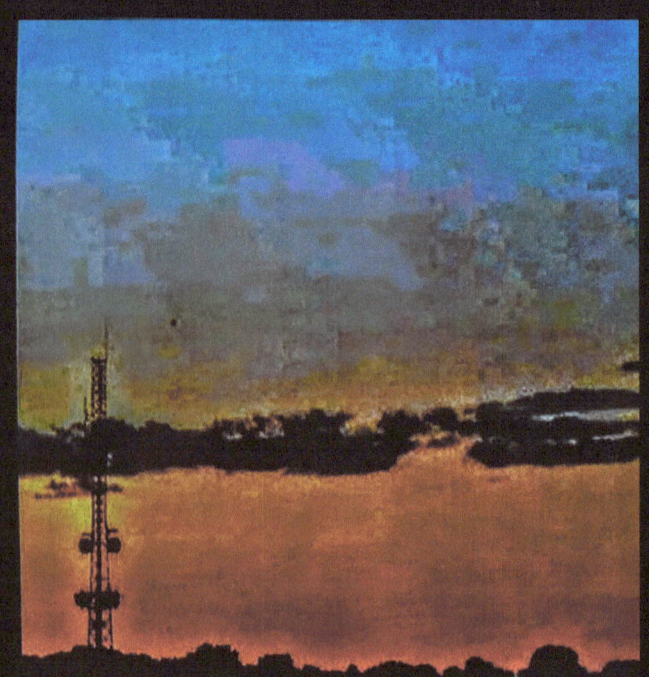
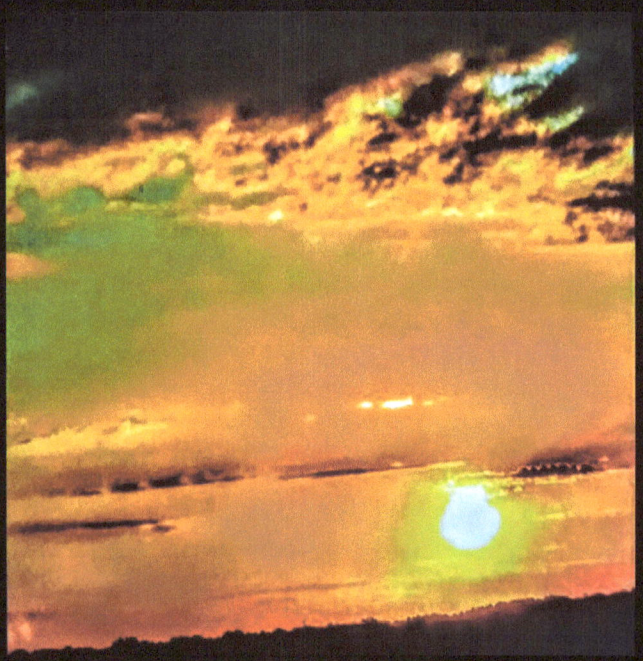

August

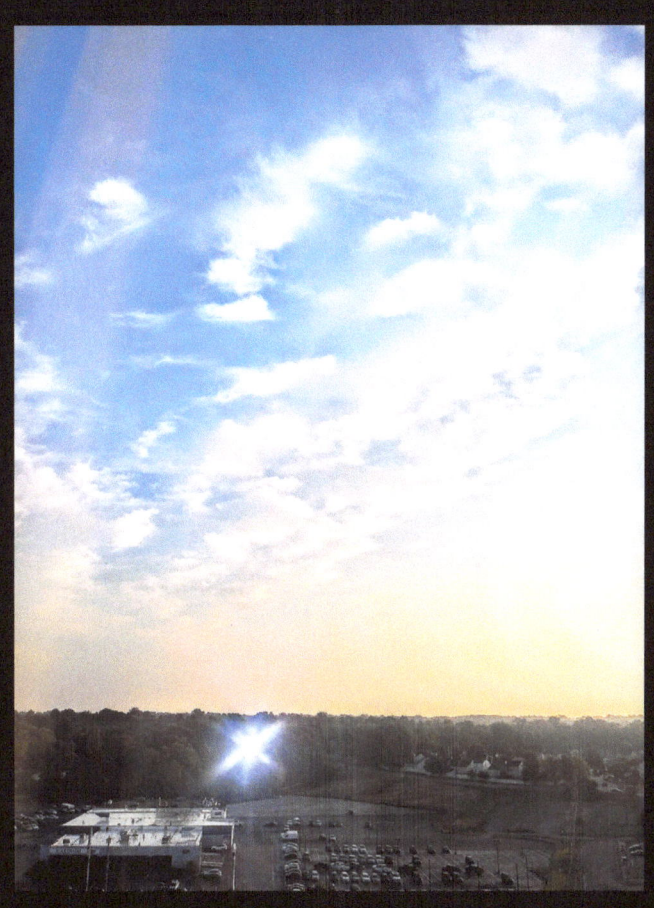
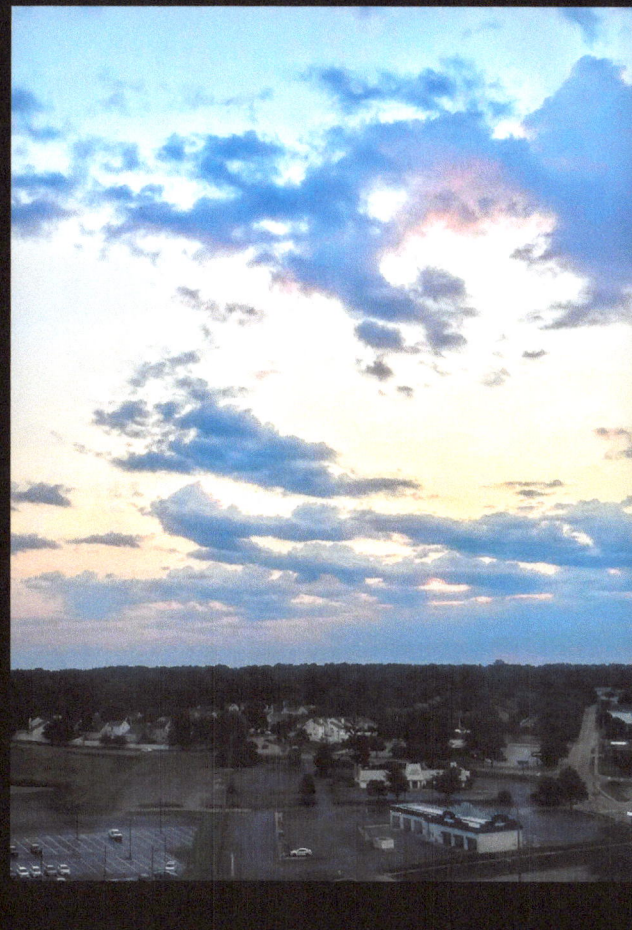

September

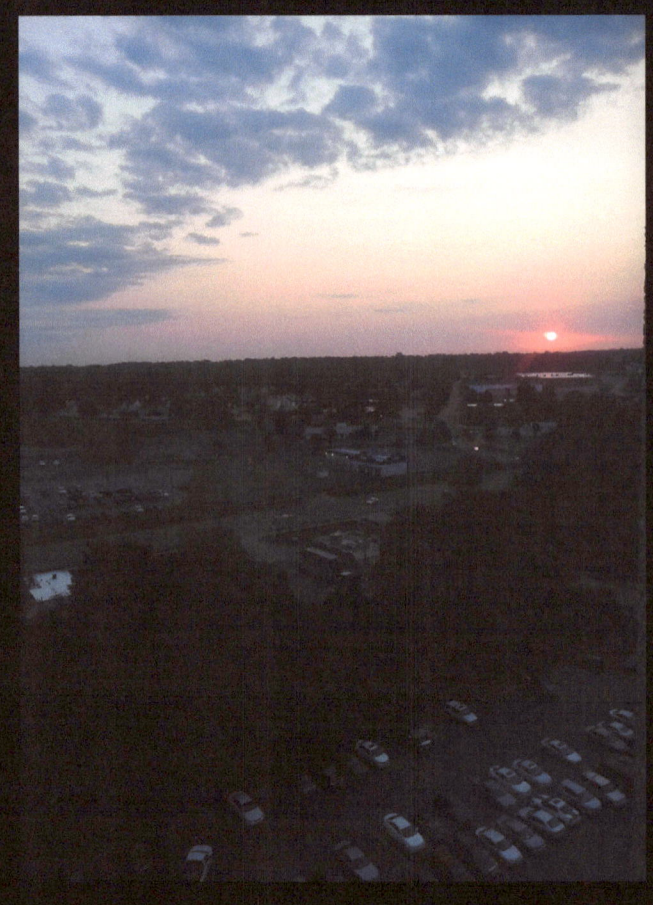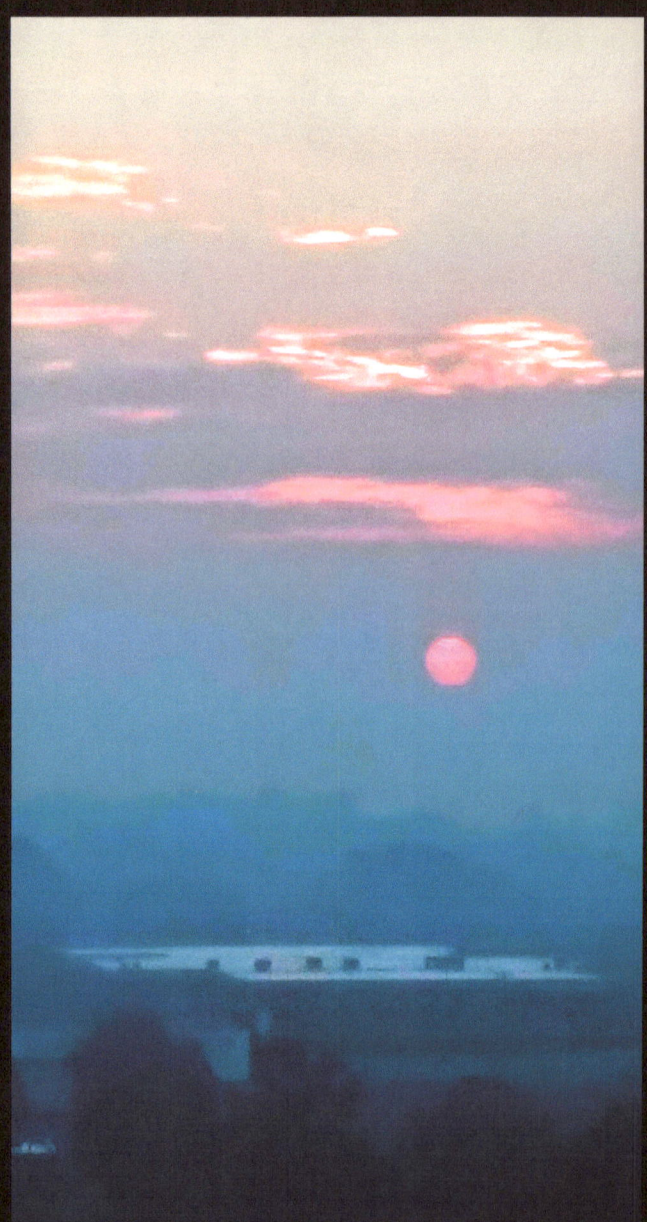

October

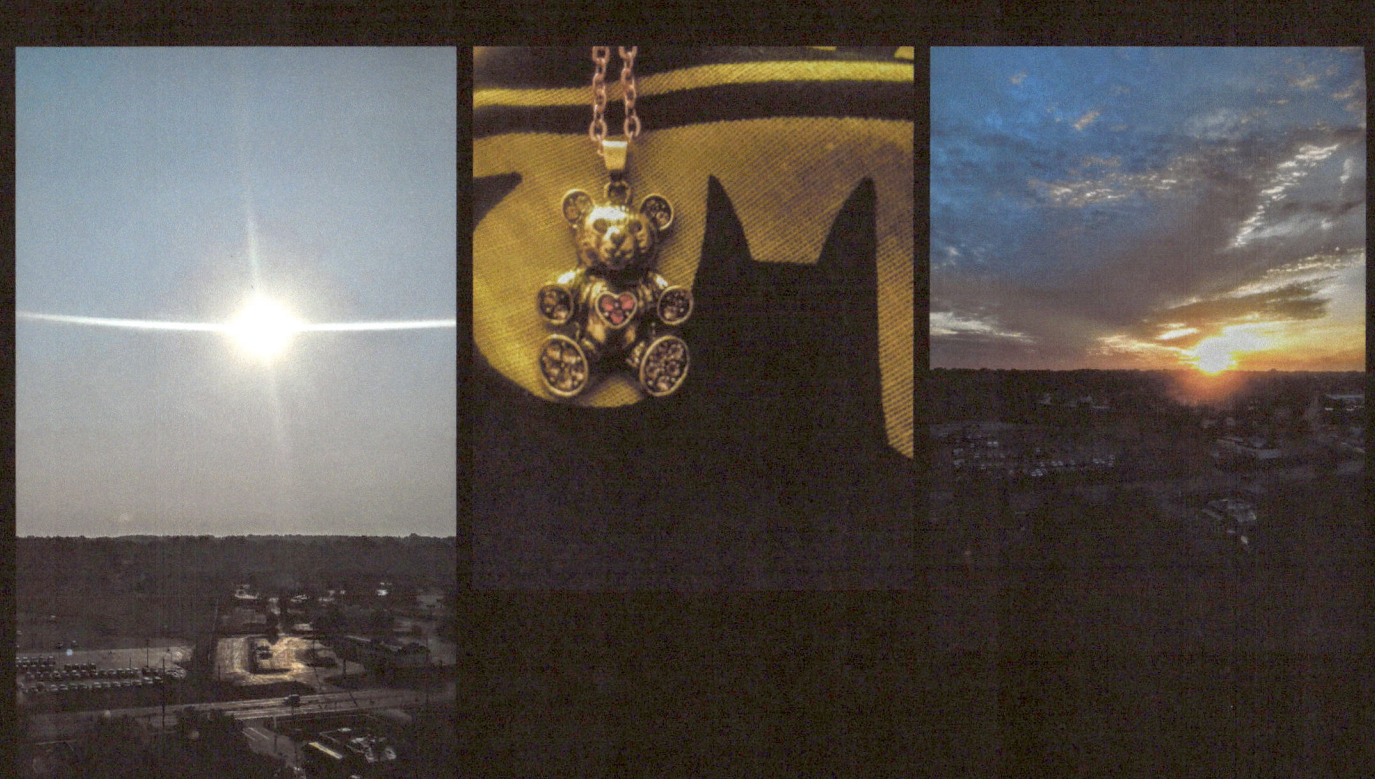

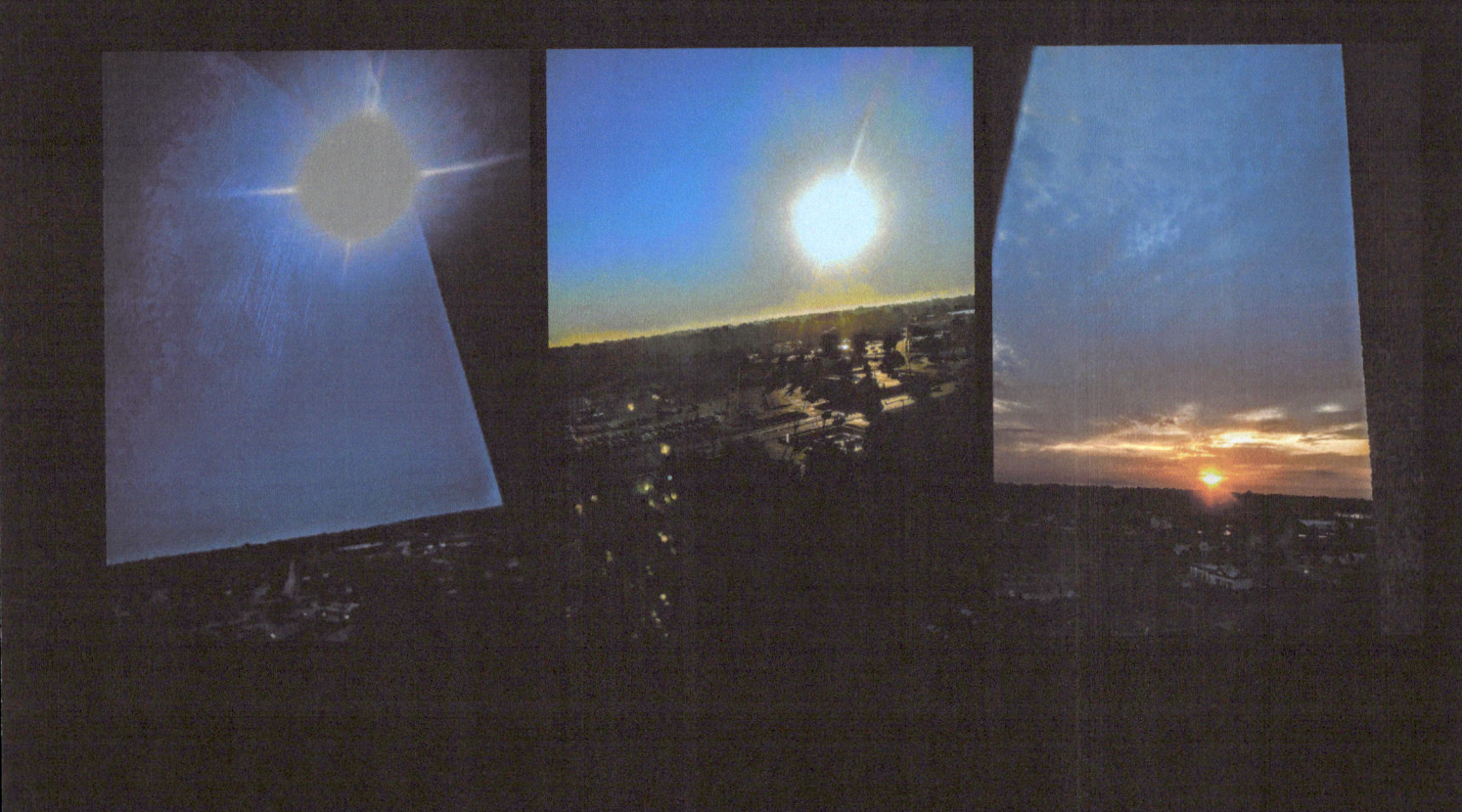

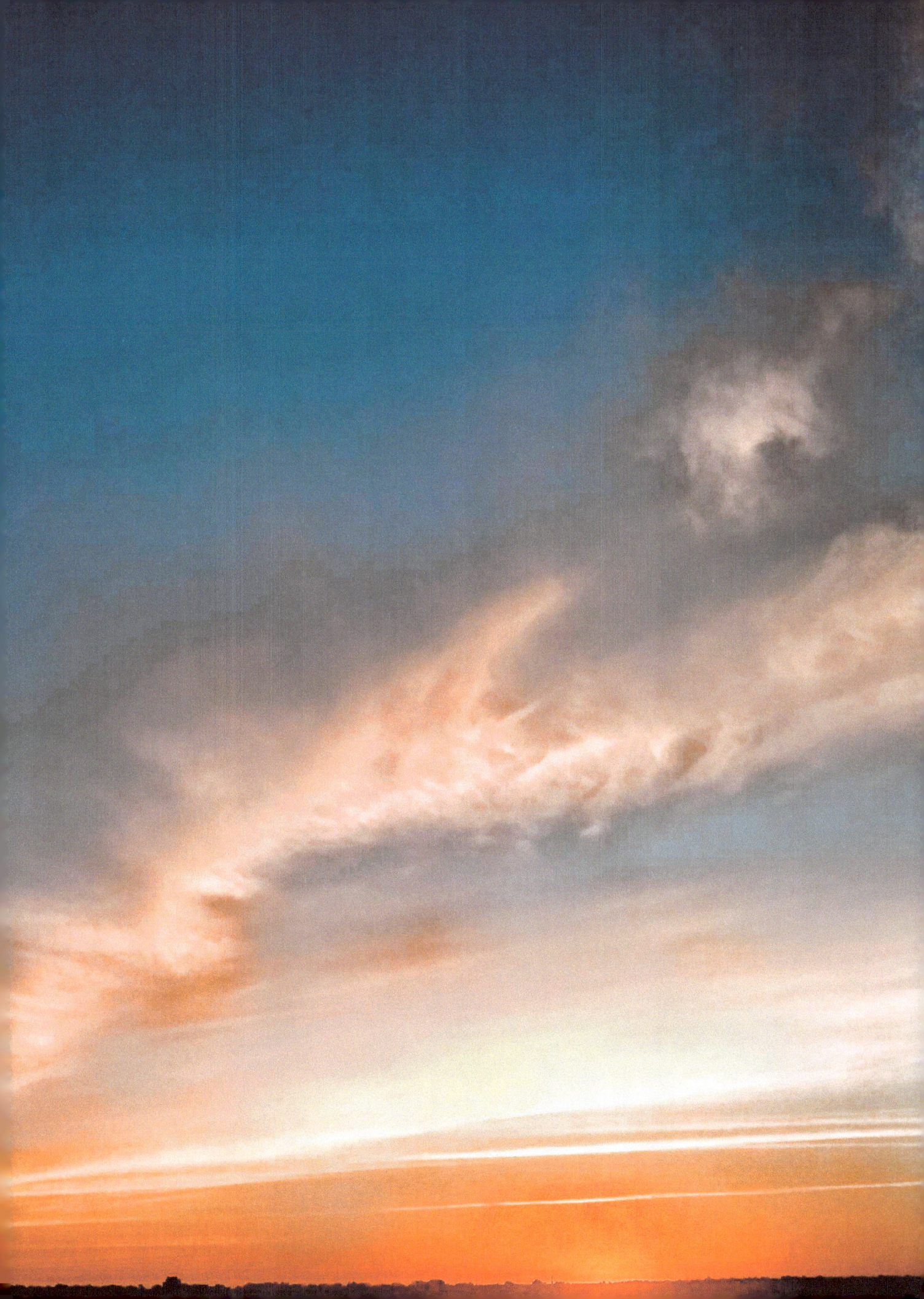

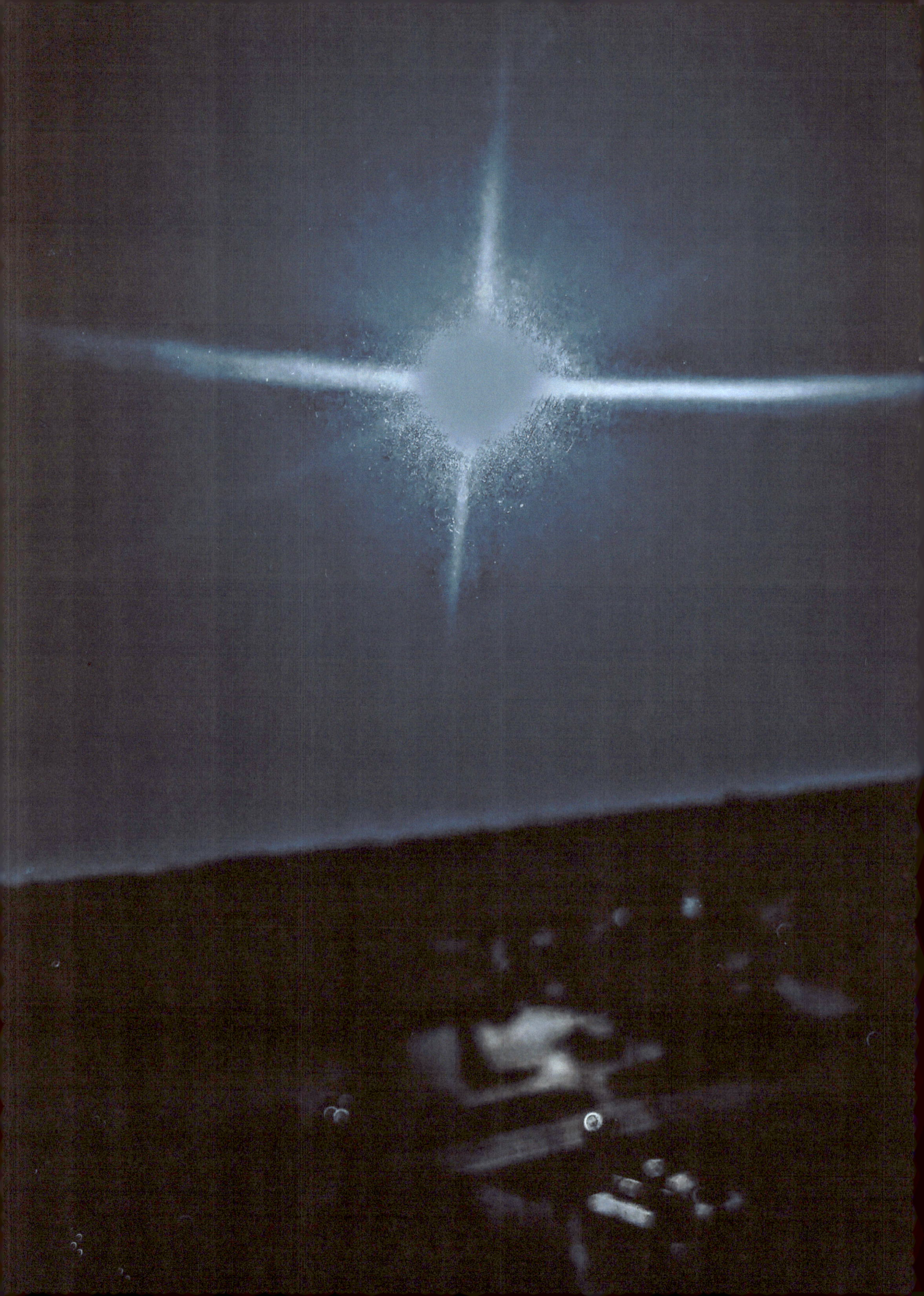

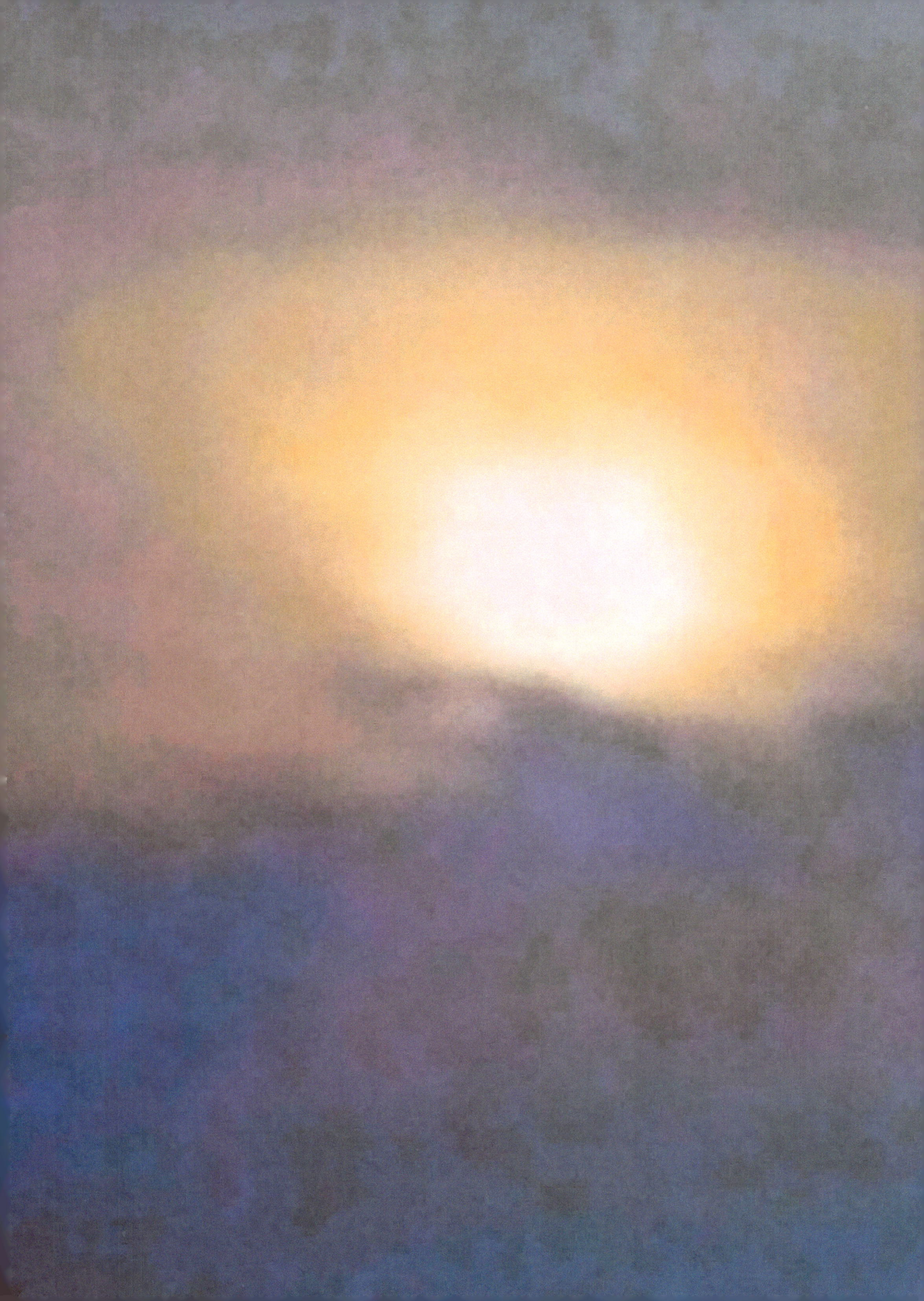

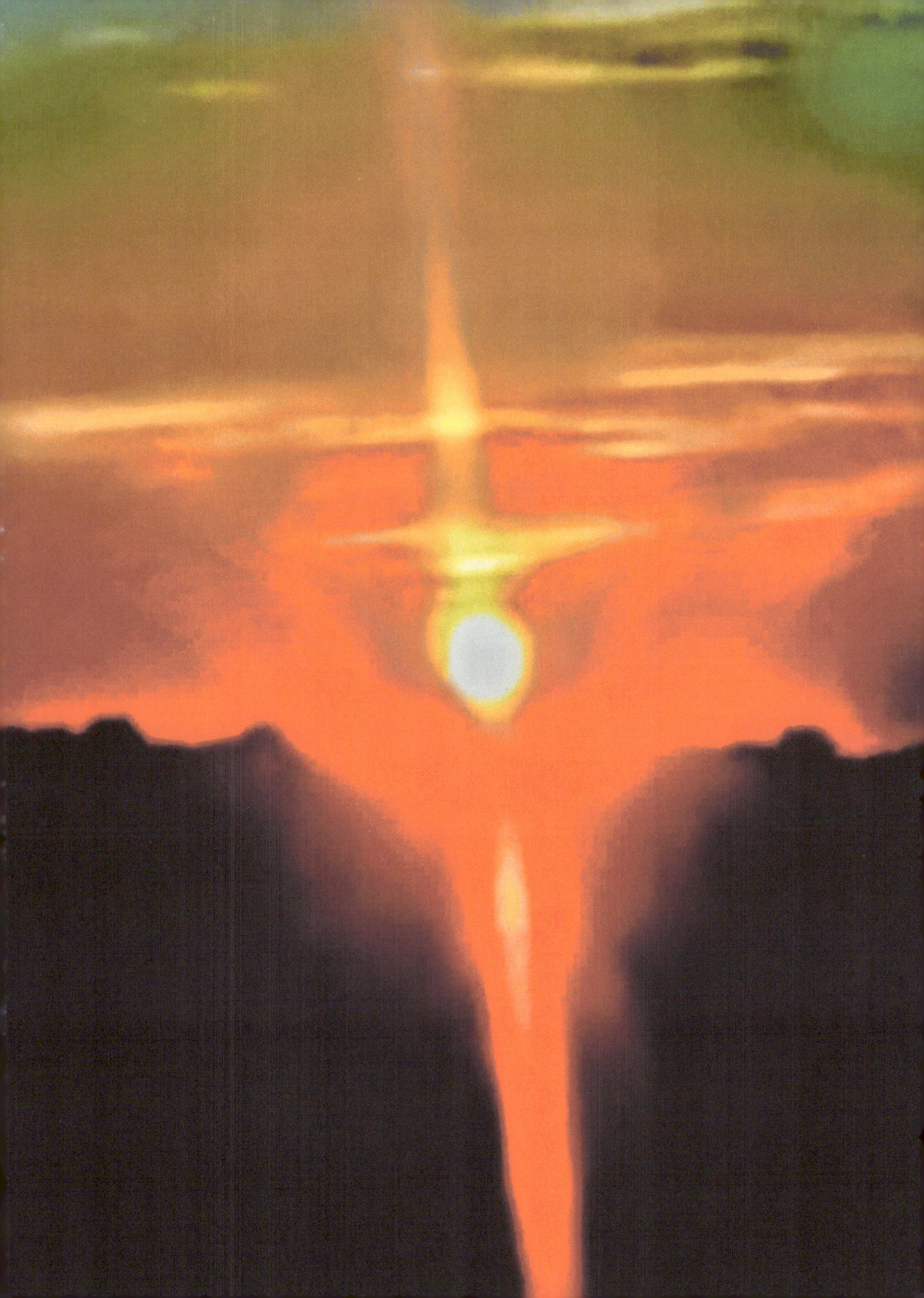

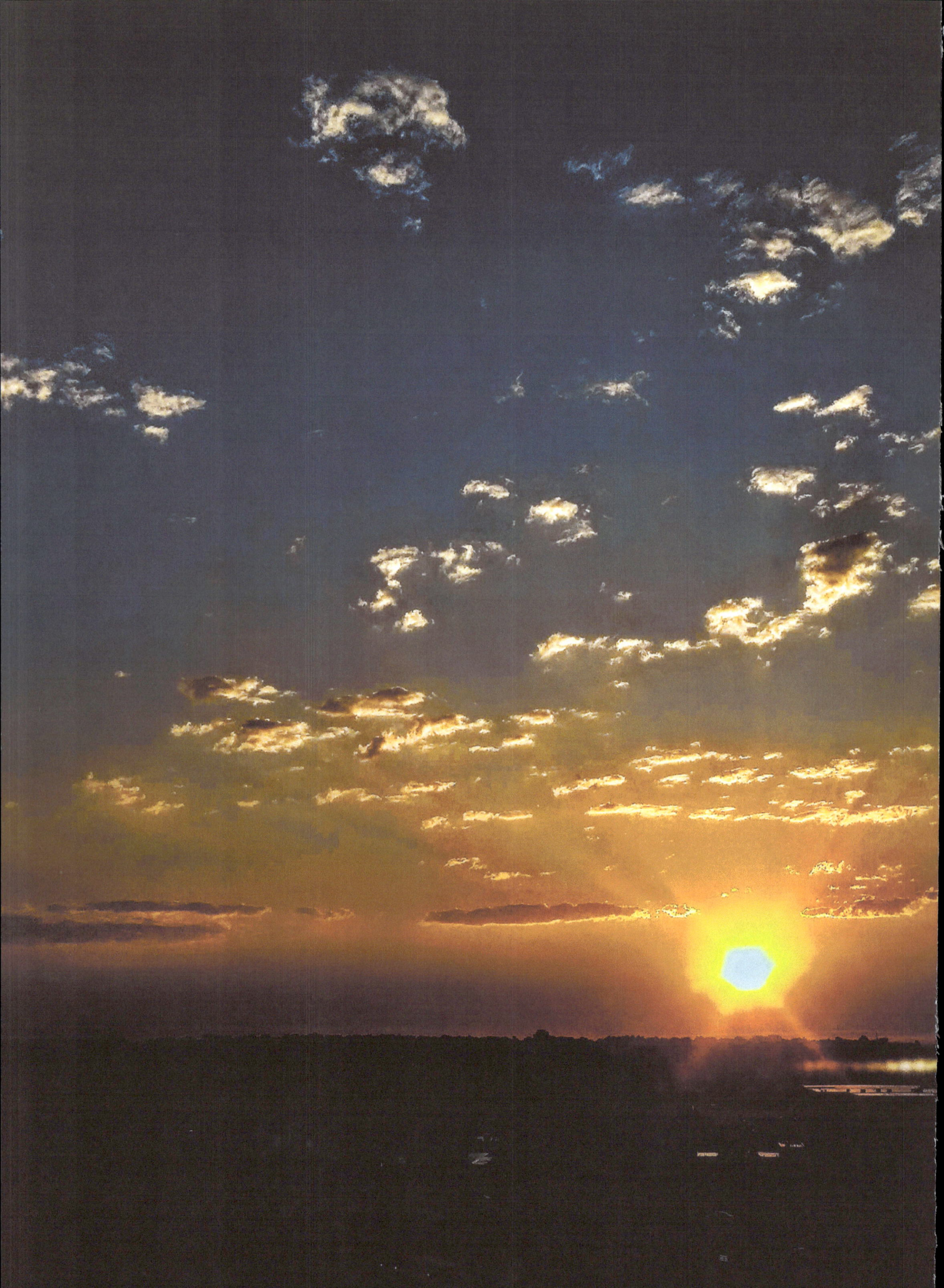

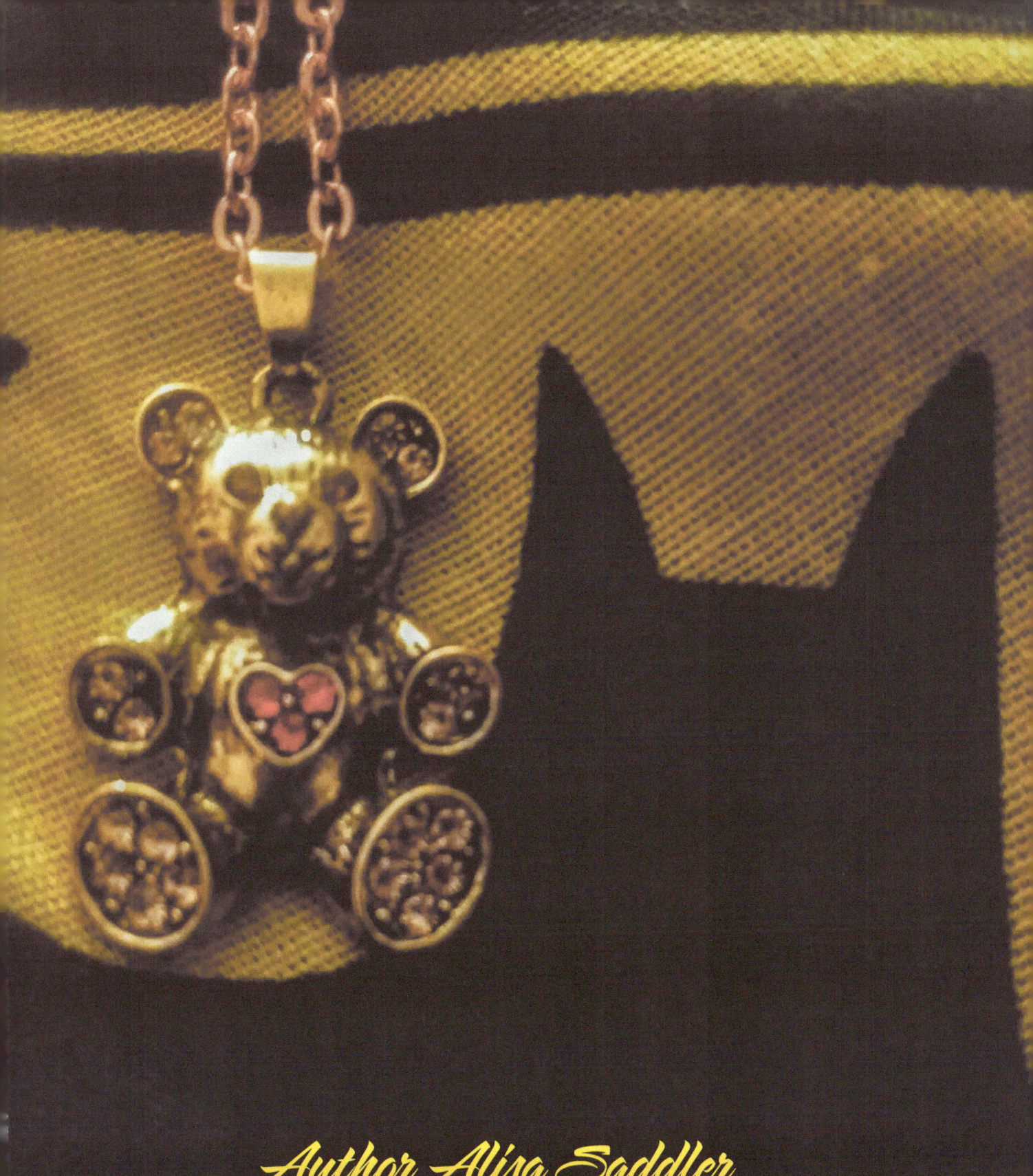

Author Alisa Saddler
Illustrator Alisa Saddler

Alisa R. Saddler holds a BFA from Fontbonne University in Saint Louis, Missouri. Alisa enjoys painting, drawing, and photography. Alisa is a paraprofessional for the Special School District through Hazelwood East High School in Hazelwood, Missouri. A Sunrise is a disc that comes above the horizontal line in the sky. Sunrise only comes in the morning only. These images enhance your imagination. In these images you will see things. Sometimes you will see people, angel, teddy-bear and more. These images can help a person psychologically and can verbally express their thoughts.

www.ingramcontent.com/pod-product-compliance
Lightning Source LLC
Chambersburg PA
CBHW051839210526
45473CB00005B/1952